Lacunae

100

IMAGINED

ANCIENT

LOVE

POEMS

DANIEL

NADLER

FARRAR

STRAUS

GIROUX

NEW

YORK

Farrar, Straus and Giroux

18 West 18th Street, New York 10011

Printed in the United States of America

First edition, 2016

Library of Congress Cataloging-in-Publication Data

Names: Nadler, Daniel J., 1983– author.

Title: Lacunae : 100 imagined ancient love poems / Daniel Nadler.

Description: First edition. | New York : Farrar, Straus and Giroux, 2016.

Identifiers: LCCN 2015035422 | ISBN 9780374182694 (hardback) |

ISBN 9780374714819 (e-book)

Subjects: | BISAC: POETRY / Ancient, Classical & Medieval.

Classification: LCC PS3614.A3844 A6 2016 | DDC 813/.6—dc23

LC record available at http://lccn.loc.gov/2015035422

Designed by Quemadura

Our books may be purchased in bulk for promotional,
educational, or business use. Please contact your local
bookseller or the Macmillan Corporate and Premium Sales
Department at 1-800-221-7945, extension 5442, or by
e-mail at MacmillanSpecialMarkets@macmillan.com.

www.fsgbooks.com
www.twitter.com/fsgbooks
www.facebook.com/fsgbooks

1 3 5 7 9 10 8 6 4 2

For Nitzan

Contents

You hear the sun in the morning
through closed shutters. As you sleep
the early sky is colored
in fish scales, and you open your eyes
like a street
already lined with fruit.

YOUR LIPS are as full as a wound
guarded in battle. Your skin is the color of my eyelids
when the sun passes through.
The sea takes my shape as I float in it
but your hair falls all around you, like the paths of gravity
made visible.

A BODY looks like an unopened bell
and long sounds called me here
but vast now and silent you are a bell
and I do not know how to hold you.

YOUR ARMS are as long as sand falling from a cracked fist.
Visible petals of a silent swelling,
you encase me in one motion
like foam whitening a planet
with the sea's final strength.

You are as happy as a waterwheel
when the earth is flooding.

Beside you I sleep with difficulty—
a cherry rolling along the stem of its thought.

Perpetual wings of the moistened eyelashes
I waited for you like vines around a house that was never built.

My lips are shy,
like a candle that will not flicker.

Ripening spots of white starlight onto our cold blue sphere,
you made the night reflect everything
in pools of water.

Even the wet streets of the planet would see me reaching for
    your hand
like a paddle returning to the surface of a lake.

THE MOON has gone farming at night
in the soil of your dreams. Tall trees
are growing there, for you to climb,
and the flower I gave you during the day
can barely break through the ground.

THE STRAWBERRY she held between her teeth
was wild, plucked; quiet. Its color
continued
into the seal of her lips.

I WOULD twist my arms like coral
if that made them delicate enough to hold you.

I WANT to boast
around you, like a horse rearing straight up
in the stars.

But I have nothing to say.
Like night
when the moon is out.

I TUGGED at your laughter like a rope
that loosened the whole knot of your skin
until all of it fell to the floor.

A SPIDER cannot be used as bait,
nor its silk as fishing wire. It will never agree to this.
Lowering itself from your finger,
making its own line down, through the water,
these are things
that even your naked body cannot effect.
Bright as it is
on the shoreline.

THE WAVE has come to collect the little ports on the coast
but it will take forever, since we are laughing.

Near twilight dust settles in a cavern above the rocks,
and a shawl conceals the purpose of the first heat.

The air is filled with feathers, and our skin
with shadows. Shall I say they are still?

I HOLD your hips
as you straddle me
like a signature
trapping white space
inside itself.

BETWEEN KISSES the air is quiet,
like trees after a snowfall. Talking softly, after,
a branch is shaken loose.

EVEN YOUR words will not leave you
now that they know
that to lighten your body
by even so much as themselves
would remove the balance
from what had been measured precisely.

ON YOUR BACK you sleep as if your wings were planted in the sand.

To THE BIRD an island is not as bright as a star.
But which can it land on?

Is the earth really bent
so gradually
that we can make a bed anywhere?

Not in the dark-skinned sea, or in night,
which fills the shape of your mouth
until your face is bloated,
like something newly born.

So we plant ourselves in some clearing, in a forest,
until our bodies break like seeds at night—
until a white tentacle, as tender as a root,
grows in a glass of water.

THE GROUND of the forest has become muddy in the rain
and now it looks as though we will not find the earrings
your sister gave you. Where did we first lie down?
The whole earth
seems to bear the imprint
of our bodies.

Love,
the skeleton of a ship on the seabed
takes water as its flesh
and maybe schools of fish
as momentary sails. A single pearl
lost to a current
can become to it
a navigable star.

THIS GIRL'S words are as ordered
as birds in the sky when there are fish below.
What is she saying to me?

THE EARTH was fruit, and stars, and motion.
Your mouth was sticky. And your sight
flew in all the directions of birds.
There was no need for music.
So which devil taught you, sweet girl,
to close your eyes when you kiss?

You DISAPPEAR beside me in a forest. Walking,
I cannot hear
the moment when fewer leaves are crushed,
and I speak to you
as if it made no difference that the forest listened in your
    place.

For you I learned
that what is near us is never what is near us.

COLOR IS sleeping in some birds
when the sun is too early
to make use of it.

WHAT WILL you do with these pearls he has given you?
Can you eat them? Can you grind them into honey
and return them to the water, sweeter than they were?
Your neck is not a graveyard for the sea.
So don't become a ghost
that scares away
the fish you must catch for your parents.

SHE UNDRESSED in the deep shadows of the garden she
    loved.
Swans meandered through branches,
and pecked at black pillars
still warm from ancient times. Hornets swarmed
around a dethroned king. And she had not yet told him.

Apart from you I am as lost
as a pattern in marble.
The delicate hairs
of the stone
were left behind
by your own soft body.

WHEN the sun is wide and drying and filled
with the soft light that snares
the evening mind of life, no feet
will find the spot where a tiger
leapt back and forth
over the rose it worshipped.

*

THE SEASON is yet unlit
by the glint of the sewing needle.
The thread is stored away, the light
is an unwoven shirt.

A GLACIER glows pink
from the sun it encases
in its ice. This is what is told
about time.

HOUSE, floating under moon
on a river. Propelled by silver oars
held from dark windows.
Blankets, covers, and sheets
raised as a sail.

ON MAPS the sea carries color.
But a swarm of shadowed fish
under the surface,
like moving marble,
eats the colored bits, gradually.
One day maps will show this.

Birds aglow in yellow do not carry ashes.
What the river carries, their talons cannot trap
and even sand slips through. Where the river narrows
ashes splash together, making the shapes they were.

THE STAR has given me a body:
an empty room
without windows.

Soil guards the sleep
of plant roots. When we pull them
they taste soft, like night.

THICK IN the forest masks are hung in rows, grinning.
The underside of a dripping leaf is dry.
Dawn is still pinned under the black body of night that fell
    asleep on top of us.
The cackle of thunder, like a puzzle, summons the spiders
    in the canopy.
A nest of stone birds is getting wet.
The drumming of fish, thrashing in a canoe, consecrates
    the rain.
Charcoaled trees burn slowly, to tease the lightning.
But the underside of a dripping leaf is dry.

THE SUN began eating
the parts of the fruit
exposed to air.

What was lodged in dark soil
would stay whole. Until the panther
dug it up with its paw
and sliced away the poison half
with its nail.

By the evening your hair is curled
like the new tentacles of an octopus. You move
where the light of the surface
has set.

APPROACH shadows like shallow water
into which you can reach
and touch indigo reefs.

WHEN YOU slipped off your dress, orders streamed from
    your lips
like a waterfall
that birds think they can land on.
Your cheeks maddened with color, your breasts
accusatory, you looked at me as though I knew
I could never lower your eyes in the morning.

THE PIGMENT of crushed petals
was smeared along both sides
of the bird's beak.
But its wings were still limp enough
to drag along the ground.

I EMBRACED YOU by mistake
when I was only trying to caress you.
Now you love me.

COOKING under some trees
you must break the salt necklace
and let its white beads
fall into the iron pan.
Rain in the glint of an eclipse.

Your dark breasts glow,
the pan crackles.

LIKE the wind that gusts coastal pines toward the water
sleep bends me toward my lover
and I cannot drink from her.

I GUARDED your sleep like a young cat
who hunts down dreams
that climb out of the floorboards
in the dead of midnight. I'm sorry I found it hard to stay
    awake
during breakfast.

IF YOU stand there in the open rain
and cup your breasts in your hands
the stream of the sky cannot take its course
around your whole skin.

You were always modest like that, leaving something
even to the imagination of water.

But what is left for me
to not know of you?

Need I open a sky
to find the last soft shame
in your nakedness?

YOUR HEAD seems lower in this light
as you try to dry fish with your candle
at nightfall. You should not have spent the day
sleeping on my chest. Your skin is too young
for a man caked in salt. Happy as you were
on my hill of nets.

My love, they will always seem like a hammock to you
at noon,
when I return.

THE still
shadowed
sand.

Impatient for heat.
The fatigue of a shell
from keeping its arch.

No longer than a beach
can I wait for you
to become naked.

FRESH BANANA LEAVES can carry whole fish
across the surface of the ocean
when they are too tired to swim.
With your eyes half-closed
your still shaking body
wants currents
to continue the work of motion.

THE AFTERNOON is a fugitive
from the morning, and the night
is another country.

You curse the rain outside your window, believing
that it alone prevents your journey.

Your young lover, at the other end of a sea
suspended in the air
would surely understand.

AND if a bird descended on your shoulder
to whisper nothing in your ear
would you be angry? Vain beauty
that expects messages
to which it can reply.

Your hair is suspended in motion.
The silhouetted mane of a galloping horse
painted on a rock
by which it passed.

LIKE wooden planks from a broken ship
dashed against great stones,
my words you made into a spectacle
for the whole village. I only meant to tell you
I love another.

Down the river the creatures in the basin prepare
for the splashes the children will make
when they dispute their race. Stirred silt
will fill the little mouths of fish
with clay.

THE TREE collapsed on itself
leaving a pile of bark
over its roots.

What, foolish daughter,
did you think?
That it would shrink back into the ground?

THE growing fingers of clouds meet
like children
discovering they have hands.

DAUGHTER, along the rim of what you were knitting
I can see the circumference of your will.
You rarely show it,
and most often you end where you are silent.
But somehow, after the edge of this quilt
there is refusal
where there is nothing.

Why is the forest canopy strung with rope?
What have the children done with the branches?
Now the sun can only reach us through a maze.
As if it, too, had to pass through their games.

We walk around, all of us now, preparing the morning
with a grid of shadows on our skin.
As if we only escaped sleep
illicitly, the print of its servitude
still on us.

It was a cold morning on the forest floor, and wet.
And now, waking to a canopy of ropes,
as if the tree trunks were spiders' legs at night
needling a web around us in the air,
we, awaking already within its mouth . . .

The old man has gone back to sleep another night.
What have the children done with the branches?

THE BIRD is in the center of the sun.
Its outline is silent,
as its nude, smooth wings extend
across the sphere of light.
They almost block it.

I can never tell
which part of nature is posturing:
To the sun the bird becomes a wall of glass,
its eyes, at the top of its silhouette,
pass pure light—
the fire of the underworld
seen through a slit between two stones.

AFTER two days I was luminous and half-naked
under the crow, the sky
was his company and he was mine, tied
to the air as I was to this earth, bitter, enraged, I drowned
my legs in water I could not reach, my mouth
is dry but the crow loves me, this morning, his shriek has
    authority.

THE ANIMALS were slowly digging in the mud, and were
   frightened.
Laughter was the refuge of the weather, and hunger
sounded like water that had nowhere to drain. More water
was found under the mud, digging.

WE CAME across a hunter disguised as a bird.
The towns pay these lords for protection. This is revealed
in a parable the women tell. They speak of a rose
that grew in the desert from a drop of blood.

THE DANCING GIRL has veiled her body
in movement. Drums grunt like voices
calling for water in the sun.
Dripping onto the hot skin of a drum
droplets would also dance
until they soaked up the sound.

THIS SLIM BODY of yours
is covered in feathers,
as if someone intended to hunt you.

Under this sun
you cannot be comfortable. Girl of high birth
let me make bedding
of your clothes. I have nothing to sleep on
and no other excuse
to offer you.

A TEAR was painted on your cheek
without ceremony. It looks like a mountain falling
down your face, and was meant to weigh as much
in your heart. Yet there is no sadness in you
as you sit beside me,
and place another log in the fire.

AT the bottom of the pond in your heart
there is no silt
to stir. Your eyes, wide and clear,
are made of ocean.

IF I CAN deceive this girl then let me
forge mountains
hard enough to echo the words they're made of.
Let me blink, and undo myself for long enough
to notice I am gone.

You TELL ME I have pine needles for bedding
and expect me to go home. Sweet girl,
if your pillow were the moving water of a creek
I would lie down beside you and ask the fish
to only nibble at our hair
until the water cooled our dreams.

THEY DO NOT want to be noticed
among so many burning things.
Their kiss,
as quiet as the sound left by an ink brush
moistened by water,
recording nothing.

A RIVER has gotten away from you. Pools are forming at your feet. Now night opens you.

ONLY THIS MUCH do I know:
When he came to me I was naked,
though I waited for him dressed.
As if the clothes themselves
were afraid of him. All the strings of my undergarments,
and even my belt:
snakes sliding down
from a tree.

ON YOUR body I left behind
the fading moisture of a kiss.

Weightless as a sewing needle
resting on your skin.

You don't want to move
because it will roll off of you.

WHY HAVE my friends spoken of him
as if he were a spider, and my love
the silk of his web? Every word he speaks
weighs so much in my ear, how could he have anything left
    in him
to make silk?

YOUR thin body, encased in my warmth
like a wick in a flame
feeding my light
consumes you.

BROTHER,
ever since your promise that one day
you would return to marry her,
her thin body has grown thinner
under her glowing skin,
like a shipwreck trapped in the closed bulb of a new flower.
The spine of its keel is almost bulging
through the petal.
When are you coming?

WHAT IS this belt made of, that clasps your dress to your
    waist?
Could a bird not carry it away, easily? And your shoulders,
on which this dress hangs—are they wide enough to hold it
if you shrug?

ARE YOU the same girl who sheltered the sun in her hair when the night made no room for it? You walked around all night, in the kitchen, trying not to wake anyone—trying to cover your head with your arms.

WHO ARE you going to meet tonight
in the tall grass
where even snakes cannot find each other?

Your bare feet
will be the safest part of you.

THE RAIN kisses my face
without your permission. The sun
heats my skin, the wind
tightens it. So what do you have to say to me?

A LAMB blinking over a patch of earth
does not know what you have done. Feed it,
and it will eat from your hand
as if you wore the skin of a washed grape.

My tigers have left me.
I awake too late in the day, after a heavy rain
has played its notes on my roof.
I don't even tie them to anything.

THE MAN who grows flowers in a field
for lovers to give to one another
is not himself lonely.

He left last winter to see his brother,
and now his field is wild.

He is not kept company by the wind,
and dawn alone does not steady his heart.
All the elements in the mountain pass
do make their way into the soil,
but he sleeps at night in a bed
beside a woman, and is as dreamless as a goat.

HAIR covered a face
the way old vines conceal a door.
The iron eyes of an owl
open at me
like ornaments from a mother's home
familiar from youth.

CLAY pots, shaped from the inside
like a sun
when the sky was spinning.

THE red earth changes color when a stream runs over it
and you have become darker since you married. Sister,
even the woven strength of youth
cannot protect you from boredom.
You used to follow close behind me
as we raced against the stream.

YOUR husband is stretched out on the ground
as if he were listening for something.
Ask him to come back to the table.
Whatever was there is now here.

THE GIRL cries from the number of fingers and toes
she cannot yet count. Sister, the terror
at this immense nudity of unknowing
will in time subside
like a sea burying a billion colored corals with its name.

BROTHER, don't look away when she glances at you,
and stop trying to find omens in the syllables of her name.
Go up to her, and say out loud
the name of our father, and if your voice doesn't break
she may even see something of his face
in yours.

Even as you look at her
across the vessel of wine
her parents will pour,
love will take time to reach her,
like light—
tracing the work of dawn
as she sleeps.

On another world
large tree ferns
descend toward the sea
from moist valleys.
Overhead, our star,
exploding
like the radiating veins of a halved grapefruit.

As THE village goes up
in smoke
a dry cloud is rotating overhead,
fed like a whirlpool
in the sky.

We press our hands together.
It is better to be
together in life, willingly,
than by any force.

His limbs covered in sweat, and ash;
his hair the way it was before it ever grew—
this was your husband, after the fire
that even ate water.

Do not wail, young sister,
for he wielded the buckets as if they were weapons
and fought as if the forest were no less his home
than our village.

SISTER, when you look at him
with your black-rimmed eyes,
let the sun's rays
speak for your mouth. Light knows
what to say of him.

A SAND dune came toward us like a sailing ship
made of stone
that was breaking in the wind.

WHEN the strange rain singed the outline of a lake into
    the sand
we left flowers at every spot where a fish would perish.
The sand turned to glass, and white in the sun
the glass spread the sun like a chant.

I HAVE never seen improvements to the flesh. If a man
    should steal, let it be sugarcane
to redden his tongue like a guilty ox. And let it be the holiest
    light
to strike the shadows from his mouth. Speech cannot find its
    way out in that darkness.
And let it be rice, to sleep on. And let it be
a woman; green and white as bamboo and milk:
a smooth stone
to set upon the chest.
For I have never known improvements to the flesh.

ISLANDS are pronounced by the ocean without bubbles.
Sometimes the ocean chokes on an island
as it tries to take it back;
these are left alone.

These are left alone
to defy the heat and the birds,
and when bubbles appear around them
they harden into reefs.
Such islands the ocean can no longer pronounce.
Their names push back the language of the water: a beach.

Leave me a stone
from the towering mountain
that once was still growing in the sea.

Leave me the moon
to reflect certainty
the way a child's face reflects its mother.

And leave me your black shadow
so it can absorb
the light that claims you are gone.

AND SO

I envisioned a woman stepping out of the ocean wearing
every starfish at once, like armor.

I crystallized my eyes with the liquor of the seed I
planted in my mouth.

I cut my destiny in two and kept the heavier one.

*

Acknowledgments

Thank you to Jorie Graham—my mentor.

I wish to express gratitude to the editors of the following journals, in which these poems originally appeared, some in slightly different form:

CALVIN BEDIENT, *Lana Turner*:

"After two days I was luminous and half-naked"; "The afternoon is a fugitive"; "By the evening your hair is curled"; "The ground of the forest has become muddy in the rain"; "If I can deceive this girl then let me"; "Love"; "What is this belt made of, that clasps your dress to your waist?"

TIMOTHY DONNELLY, *Boston Review*:

"A tear was painted on your cheek"; "And if a bird descended on your shoulder"; "Apart from you I am as lost"; "Brother"; "Color is sleeping in some birds"; "Down the river the creatures in the basin prepare"; "The earth was fruit, and stars, and motion"; "Like the wind that gusts coastal pines toward the water"; "Thick in the forest masks are hung in rows, grinning"; "This girl's words are as ordered"; "This slim body of yours"

BIN RAMKE, *Denver Quarterly*:

"A body looks like an unopened bell"; "At the bottom of the pond in your heart"; "The growing fingers of clouds meet"; "House, floating under moon"; "I have never seen improvements to the flesh. If a man should steal, let it be sugarcane"; "Islands are pronounced by the ocean without bubbles"; "On your back you sleep as if your wings were planted in the sand"; "The star has given me a body"; "The wave has come to collect the little ports on the coast"; "We came across a hunter disguised as a bird"; "When the sun is wide and drying and filled"

BRADFORD MORROW, *Conjunctions*:

"A glacier glows pink"; "A lamb blinking over a patch of earth"; "The animals were slowly digging in the mud, and were frightened"; "As the village goes up"; "Approach shadows like shallow water"; "A sand dune came toward us like a sailing ship"; "Between kisses the air is quiet"; "The bird is in the center of the sun"; "Birds aglow in yellow do not carry ashes"; "Brother, don't look away when she glances at you"; "Cooking under some trees"; "The dancing girl has veiled her body"; "Daughter, along the rim of what you were knitting"; "Even your words will not leave you"; "Hair covered a face"; "I want to boast"; "Like wooden planks from a broken ship"; "The man who grows flowers in a field"; "The moon has gone farming at night"; "My tigers have left me"; "On maps the sea carries color"; "The pigment of crushed petals"; "The season is yet unlit"; "Soil guards the sleep"; "The sun began eating"; "The tree collapsed on itself"; "To the bird an island is not as bright as a star"; "What will you do with these pearls he has given you?"; "Who are you going to meet tonight"; "Why is the forest canopy strung with rope?"; "You disappear beside me in a forest. Walking"; "You curse the rain outside your window, believing"; "You hear the sun in the morning"; "Your lips are as full as a wound"

DONALD REVELL, *Colorado Review*:

"When the strange rain singed the outline of a lake into the sand"